VIRTUES FOR DISCIPLES

TRUST
Confidence in the God of Salvation

John F. Craghan

Little Rock
Scripture Study

*A ministry of the Diocese of Little Rock
in partnership with Liturgical Press*

Nihil obstat: Jerome Kodell, OSB, *Censor librorum*
Imprimatur: ✢ Anthony B. Taylor, Bishop of Little Rock, January 27, 2016

Cover design by Ann Blattner. Cover photo: Lightstock. Used with permission.

Photos: pages 6, 8, 14, 17, 18, 19, 23, 25, 29, 32, 35, Thinkstock Images by Getty. Used with permission.

ISBN: 978-0-8146-3689-3 (print); 978-0-8146-3690-9 (ebook)

Contents

Introduction

Alive in the Word brings you resources to deepen your understanding of Scripture, offer meaning for your life today, and help you to pray and act in response to God's word.

Use any volume of **Alive in the Word** in the way best suited for you.

- **For individual learning and reflection,** consider this an invitation to prayerfully journal in response to the questions you find along the way. And be prepared to move from head to heart and then to action.
- **For group learning and reflection,** arrange for three sessions where you will use the material provided as the basis for faith sharing and prayer. You may ask group members to read each chapter in advance and come prepared with questions answered. In this kind of session, plan to be together for about an hour. Or, if your group prefers, read and respond to the questions together without advance preparation. With this approach, it's helpful to plan on spending more time for each group session in order to adequately work through each chapter.

- **For a parish-wide event or use within a larger group,** provide each person with a copy of this volume, and allow time during the day for quiet reading, group discussion and prayer, and then a final commitment by each person to some simple action in response to what he or she learned.

This volume is one of several volumes that explore the theme **Virtues for Disciples**. Each of us is called to be a disciple, a follower of Christ. The life of a disciple is challenging but it is the most fulfilling way to live. Called by name by the God who created us, we are shaped by the teachings of Christ and continually guided by the Holy Spirit. As we grow more deeply into this identity as disciples of Jesus Christ, we discover the valuable virtues that mark God's people.

The Pilgrim's Song of Trust

Begin by asking God to assist you in your prayer and study. Then read through Psalm 121, one of the psalms that pilgrims prayed as they approached Jerusalem.

Psalm 121
¹A song of ascents.

I raise my eyes toward the
    mountains.
    From whence shall come my
      help?
²My help comes from the LORD,
  the maker of heaven and earth.
³He will not allow your foot to slip;
  or your guardian to sleep.
⁴Behold, the guardian of Israel
  never slumbers nor sleeps.
⁵The LORD is your guardian;
  the LORD is your shade
  at your right hand.
⁶By day the sun will not strike you,
  nor the moon by night.
⁷The LORD will guard you from all evil;
  he will guard your soul.

[8]The Lord will guard your coming and going
  both now and forever.

After a few moments of quiet reflection on Psalm 121, consider some background information offered in "Setting the Scene."

Setting the Scene

The book of Psalms is a collection of collections of prayers. Psalm 121 belongs to one such collection (120–134) known as the "songs of ascents." These prayers were probably used by pilgrims as they went up or "ascended to" Jerusalem or as they took part in some celebration of a Jewish feast. Although this collection contains different types or genres of psalms, it does possess some common characteristics. Overwhelming trust in God, hopeful requests for forgiveness, and gratitude for the Lord's bounty toward his people typify this collection. Here the psalmist selects a simple notion or image and proceeds to develop it with an economy of words. These psalms are not cerebral.

On the contrary, they are lyrical, attempting to capture a significant image that compels one to follow attentively and prayerfully. These images often touch upon ordinary, routine matters of daily life, such as the significance of spouse and family and the centrality of the home.

The psalms are forms of Hebrew poetry in which symbolism plays a vital role. Their imagery appeals to the imagination and leads one to see God, oneself, and reality from a variety of vantage points. As poetry, they tease the reader

How does the use of symbolism and imagery help you to speak to God in prayer?

to set aside objective canons of prose and indulge oneself in the provocative and many-sided glimpses of the symbolic world. Such a world provides not only tempting delights but also stringent demands.

Understanding the Scene Itself

The entire psalm will be considered a few verses at a time. The occasional questions in the margin (as above) are for discussion with others. If you are using these materials on your own, use the questions for personal reflection or as a guide to journaling.

> ¹I raise my eyes toward the mountains.
>   From whence shall come my help?
> ²My help comes from the LORD,
>   the maker of heaven and earth.

The pilgrim begins by catching a glimpse of the mountains in the distance. At this juncture the pilgrim raises questions about his or her own personal safety as the journey is beset with perils. For example, he or she is preoccupied with the danger of stumbling on the rocky terrain. This naturally prompts the pilgrim to seek help. The security provided by the hill country on the way to the Jerusalem temple (see 1 Kgs 20:23) piques the pilgrim's interest. The mountains, therefore, offer a military and strategic sense of relief. However, the pilgrim moves from this objective sense of defense to a personal issue. His help will come from the Lord himself who resides in the temple within the holy city of Jerusalem. With the Lord there is always an abundance of help. ("Help" often has a military connotation as in "help and shield" [see Deut 33:29; Pss 33:20; 115:9-11].)

"The maker of heaven and earth" functions as more than a passing nod to God's work "in the beginning" as in Genesis 1. "Heaven and earth" is a merism, that is, an expression that combines different elements to represent a whole series. "Heaven and earth," therefore, stands for the universe. As the prophet Isaiah has particularly elaborated, creation is not a divine enterprise consigned only to the beginning. Rather, creation is an ongoing reality—God continues to create and resolve the crises of both Israel and the individual believer.

The pilgrim, therefore, in Psalm 121, does not employ an aimless epithet in addressing the Lord as "the maker of heaven and earth." The pilgrim's God is one with credentials who has intervened creatively in the past and can do so again.

When has an appreciation for creation led you to a deeper sense that God is worthy of your trust?

³He will not allow your foot to slip;
    or your guardian to sleep.
⁴Behold, the guardian of Israel
    never slumbers nor sleeps.

Given the terrain, the pilgrim can easily experience the danger of slipping. Ever alert, however, the Lord offsets this danger by assuring the traveler of constant protection. As Psalm 66:8-9 notes, the psalmist calls upon his audience to break out in praise of his God "[w]ho has kept us alive / and not allowed our feet to slip." The Lord's persistent care, therefore, more than meets the challenges of the rocky terrain.

Verse 4 introduces the overriding motif in this psalm, namely, guarding. The noun "guardian" and the verb "guard" occur a total of six times. This reassuring image recalls God's protection of the people of Israel on their perilous journey in the exodus, that is, from the land of bondage to the relative security of the Promised Land. In the covenant renewal ceremony at the close of the book of Joshua the people acknowledge, "He performed those great signs before our very eyes and protected us along our entire journey and among all the peoples through whom we passed" (Josh 24:17).

What life events have made you aware of God as your guardian?

In blessing the Israelites, the priests begin their prayer with, "The LORD bless you and *keep* you!" (Num 6:24). While the ordinary setting for this blessing is the sanctuary where the Israelites are to present themselves three times a year (Exod 23:14-17; 34:22-23), the prayer requests God's guardianship in the midst of all life's concrete problems—a request that fittingly includes the pilgrim's trek to the temple to fulfill the requirement mentioned above. Such divine protection amply demonstrates the second petition of the Aaronic or priestly blessing, namely, God's shining face and accompanying graciousness.

To reassure the pilgrim of God's ongoing oversight and alertness, the psalmist asserts in verse 4 that Israel's guardian "never slumbers nor sleeps." Being awake symbolizes alertness and readiness to take action. Although certain psalms (Pss 7:7; 44:24; 59:6) beseech God to awake and intervene on behalf of the people, in this psalm there is no need. The Lord is ever vigilant, constantly ready to enter the fray and protect his people. The Lord, therefore, is unlike Jesus' disciples who fail their Master by falling asleep in the Garden of Gethsemane (Matt 26:40; Mark 14:37; Luke 22:45).

> *The Lord is ever vigilant, constantly ready to enter the fray and protect his people.*

⁵The LORD is your guardian;
  the LORD is your shade
  at your right hand.
⁶By day the sun will not strike you,
  nor the moon by night.

Verse 5 serves as the center of the entire psalm by reinforcing the predominant image of "guard/guardian." The psalmist adds to this central metaphor by developing the image of shade. In this regard Psalm 121 shares much in common with Psalm 91, another psalm of trust or confidence. In that psalm the psalmist depicts his audience as those "who abide in the shade of the Almighty" (Ps 91:1) with the assurance that the Lord dispatches his angels "to *guard* you wherever you go" (Ps 91:11).

God as shade or shadow often occurs in the formulation "in the shade/shadow of your wings" (Pss 57:2; 63:8). There are at least two explanations for such usage in Psalm 121. In the first view the wings refer to the winged creatures (the cherubim) who guard the ark of the covenant (God's throne) in the temple (Exod 25:18-22; 1 Kgs 6:23-28). Since the object of the pilgrim's journey is the temple, such an interpretation suits the context of the psalm.

How has God provided shade for you in recent years? What does that mean to you?

In the second view the wings depict God as a mighty bird, for example, an eagle that keeps constant watch over the needs of its brood, namely, the Israelites. The book of Exodus exemplifies this imagery when the Lord describes his protection of the newly arrived former slaves at Mount Sinai: "You have seen . . . how I bore you up on eagles' wings and brought you to myself" (Exod 19:4; see also Deut 32:11-12). What commends the second view is the image of personal protection that is so central to Psalm 121.

Verse 6 with its reference to day and night underlines the constancy of the Lord's ongoing solicitude. Exposure to the Palestinian sun can pose considerable danger to the traveler (see Isa 49:10). However, the psalmist rules out this danger since the Lord will prevent the sun from striking the pilgrim. In the ancient Near East the moon was often thought to cause serious problems. (See Matthew 4:24 where lunatics [from the Latin "luna" = "moon"] figure among those cured by Jesus.) Closely allied once again with Psalm 121, Psalm 91:5 also includes the dangers of the day and night.

⁷The LORD will guard you from all evil;
   he will guard your soul.
⁸The LORD will guard your coming and going
   both now and forever.

Here the psalmist reintroduces the central metaphor of "guard" no less than three times. In the first instance it is the guarding from all evil. "Evil" refers the reader back to all the dangers mentioned in the preceding verses. The God of this psalm continues to show a vested interest in all the difficulties and problems faced by the pilgrim. In the second instance the psalmist reassures the pilgrim that God will guard his or her soul. The Hebrew word translated "soul" derives from a root meaning throat. Throat is linked to breathing and the fundamental life force comes from breathing. Hence "soul" stands for life itself. Here the psalmist assures the pilgrim that God will guard his or her life or person.

In the third instance the author employs another merism, namely, coming and going (see Deut 28:6). Every departure, therefore, and every arrival come under God's close scrutiny and care. Absolutely nothing escapes his attention. As a result, the pilgrim has every reason to indulge in divine trust and confidence. "Now and forever" heightens this sense of trust and confidence by emphasizing the aspect of perpetuity.

The psalmist employs the device of inclusion to round off his composition. Inclusion is the repetition of the same word or phrase at the beginning and at the end. In verse 1 the pilgrim inquires where his help will *come* from. In verse

Consider these connections between soul and breathing. Consider too that Genesis speaks of the Creator breathing the "breath of life" into the dust of the ground to create humans (Gen 2:7). How do these images speak to you?

8 the pilgrim hears the reassuring message that God will guard both his *coming* and his *going*. Besides defining the limits of the poem, the inclusion unifies the whole composition.

To sum up, the pilgrim has raised his eyes to take in the view of the city walls and the natural defense of the surrounding mountains. His glance catches sight of the heavens and the pilgrim instantly recalls the role of the Lord as the maker of heaven and earth. The glance has functioned as the interrogator and, having reflected on the heavens, receives a totally satisfying response that the Lord will answer his or her prayer by the message of universal concern developed in the psalm as a whole. This God is indeed an involved deity who projects an image of relentless concern.

Perhaps another scenario revealing the impact of the mountains on the pilgrim is the experience of countless waves of immigrants in the past as they sailed for the first time into New York harbor and experienced the Statue of Liberty. After a long and often arduous voyage, these immigrants sense the thrill of having made it to a new homeland with the prospect of safety and ultimate success. The sight of Miss Liberty with her welcoming torch may capture the intense feelings of the pilgrim as he or she views the surrounding mountains, the defense walls of the city, and ultimately the splendor of the Jerusalem temple where the God of Israel resides. The haunting final verse of this psalm must impact and heighten one's emotions: "The LORD will guard your coming and going / both now and forever."

Praying the Word / Sacred Reading

Spend a few moments imagining what it would have been like to journey through the barrenness of the desert toward the bustling sacred city of Jerusalem. Place yourself in the scene.

- *Perhaps you are among those making the pilgrimage on foot to celebrate a religious feast. Are you young or are you one of the older members of the group? Is this your first pilgrimage or have you traveled this route before?*

- *Maybe you are a member of the military guard assigned to watch from the ancient walls as you see a band of pilgrims approach. What might capture your attention from the vantage point you choose?*

Allow those images and thoughts to emerge. What would be the value of making an ancient prayer your own prayer as you approach the city? Does it connect you with previous generations who have traveled that route?

In your own life, what previous works of God have helped you to trust in God more deeply as you make this pilgrimage we call life? Take the time to compose even a brief prayer to the God who has provided protection for you, who has led you safely through the dangers you have encountered along the way so far.

Help me, Lord, to desire your presence, and to make my way toward you among the people whom you call your own. Stir in me the memories of your guiding presence in my life and in those who have gone before me. Renew in me the ability to see your protection and, in seeing, to walk with greater confidence in your goodness and mercy.

Living the Word

Commit yourself, as the psalmist did, to acknowledging that your help comes from the Lord. Ask for an opportunity to be an instrument of God's help and protection to someone else who is doing his or her best to succeed in this world. Perhaps this person is your neighbor who has lost his or her way, a young friend who is struggling, a coworker who is weary, a parishioner who is blinded by defeat. What might you do or say to bear witness to God's help in your own life?

God's Plan
and Judah's Response

Begin by asking God to assist you in your prayer and study. Then read through Isaiah 30:8-26, a prophecy first delivered at a time when God's people were in great political and spiritual turmoil, a time that demanded a new level of trust.

Isaiah 30:8-26

⁸Now come, write it on a tablet they
    can keep,
  inscribe it on a scroll;
That in time to come it may be
  an eternal witness.
⁹For this is a rebellious people,
  deceitful children,
Children who refuse to listen
  to the instruction of the LORD;
¹⁰Who say to the seers, "Do not see";
  to the prophets, "Do not prophesy
     truth for us;
  speak smooth things to us, see
     visions that deceive!
¹¹Turn aside from the way! Get out of the path!
  Let us hear no more
  of the Holy One of Israel!"

¹²Therefore, thus says the Holy One
     of Israel:
   Because you reject this word,
And put your trust in oppression and
     deceit,
   and depend on them,
¹³This iniquity of yours shall be
   like a descending rift
Bulging out in a high wall
   whose crash comes suddenly, in an
     instant,
¹⁴Crashing like a potter's jar
   smashed beyond rescue,
And among its fragments cannot be
     found
  a sherd to scoop fire from the hearth
  or dip water from the cistern.
¹⁵For thus said the Lord GOD,
   the Holy One of Israel:
By waiting and by calm you shall be saved,
   in quiet and in trust shall be your strength.
¹⁶"No," you said,
   "Upon horses we will flee."
   Very well, you shall flee!
"Upon swift steeds we will ride."
   Very well, swift shall be your pursuers!
¹⁷A thousand shall tremble at the threat of one—
   if five threaten, you shall flee.
You will then be left like a flagstaff on a moun-
     taintop,
   like a flag on a hill.
¹⁸Truly, the LORD is waiting to be gracious to you,
   truly, he shall rise to show you mercy;
For the LORD is a God of justice:
   happy are all who wait for him!

¹⁹Yes, people of Zion, dwelling in Jerusalem,
   you shall no longer weep;
He will be most gracious to you when you cry
      out;
   as soon as he hears he will answer you.
²⁰The Lord will give you bread in adversity
   and water in affliction.
No longer will your Teacher hide himself,
   but with your own eyes you shall see your
      Teacher,
²¹And your ears shall hear a word behind you:
   "This is the way; walk in it,"
   when you would turn to the right or the left.
²²You shall defile your silver-plated idols
   and your gold-covered images;
You shall throw them away like filthy rags,
   you shall say, "Get out!"
²³He will give rain for the seed
   you sow in the ground,
And the bread that the soil produces
   will be rich and abundant.
On that day your cattle will graze
   in broad meadows;
²⁴The oxen and the donkeys that till
      the ground
   will eat silage tossed to them
   with shovel and pitchfork.
²⁵Upon every high mountain and lofty
      hill
   there will be streams of running
      water.
On the day of the great slaughter,
   when the towers fall,

²⁶The light of the moon will be like the light of
  the sun,
  and the light of the sun will be seven times
   greater,
  like the light of seven days,
On the day the L<small>ORD</small> binds up the wounds of his
  people
  and heals the bruises left by his blows.

After a few moments of quietly listening to
the Isaiah passage, consider the background
information offered in "Setting the Scene."

Setting the Scene

A first reaction to the terms "prophet" and
"prophecy" is to conjure up a world of experts
who specialize in predicting future events. However, the very etymology of these terms (to speak
on behalf of someone else) suggests a very different approach. At the expense of being overly me-
chanical one may say that prophecy consists of
these five steps: (1) experience, (2) perception, (3)
assessment, (4) reaction, and (5) communication.
Thus a prophet first *experiences* what is happen-
ing in his or her culture. A prophet next *perceives*
that something is amiss. A prophet then proceeds
to *assess* that perception against the background
of relationship with God (covenant). A prophet
then *reacts* to that value judgment, pondering it
and suffering with it. Finally a prophet *commu-*
nicates the experience, the perception, the assessment, and the reaction to the people of God.

In this whole process, biblical scholar Walter
Brueggemann identifies two modes of prophetic

communication. The first is criticizing. Here the prophet warns and chides the audience of the dangers of conformity to the currently imposed standards of thought and conduct. The prophet points out the seductive and manipulative powers that prevent people from being genuinely human. The second mode is energizing. Here the prophet must counteract the prevailing policy that assumes that things cannot be changed. In this role the prophet articulates a message of hope. This involves the retrieval of profound longing and the refusal to accept the majority pessimistic outlook as the only show in town.

In sum, the prophetic vocation demands a passionate, realistic judgment regarding God, people, and their mutual relationship (covenant).

According to the opening verse of Isaiah (1:1) the prophet was the son of Amoz and exercised his prophetic role during most of the second half of the eighth century BC. Isaiah had an overwhelming experience not simply of God's presence but precisely of God's holiness (see Isa 6:1-13).

This experience shaped his entire prophetic career as God's holiness clashed violently with his people's sinfulness (see Isa 1:4). Time and again he exploited the epithet "the Holy One of Israel" to underline the shocking clash.

During most of Isaiah's lifetime the southern kingdom of Judah with its capital Jerusalem lived under the threat of Assyrian domination.

In the passage to be considered below the prophet advised against a Judean alliance with Egypt (see Isa 19:1–20:6; 30:1-7). In 705 BC, when King Sennacherib ruled Assyria, Judah was

> Where do you see a critical conflict between our society's norms and values and those identified in God's word?

> Have you ever felt insecure or unworthy in God's presence? Did that prevent God from accepting you or using you for a greater purpose?

a vassal state that revolted against Assyrian power. The resulting devastation in Judah was catastrophic. Only Jerusalem was left and the Judean king (Hezekiah) surrendered in 701 BC. In Isaiah's view any coalition against Assyria denied the role of the Lord's power in determining the outcome. The prophet was keenly aware that Assyria was strong enough to remain in control.

The passage to be considered below reflects the topsy-turvy period of 705–701 BC. It points to a choice between two plans: (1) the Lord's plan for Judah's well-being and (2) Judah's own machinations in a plan for well-being that cannot possibly succeed. The passage consists of various Isaian traditions that scribes and editors organized over the years. In studying these traditions, the reader must always realize that prophets speak in the language of poetry. Therefore, symbols and images serve as the conductors of their message.

Understanding the Scene Itself

The entire passage will be considered a few verses at a time. The occasional questions may be used in group discussion or for your own personal reflection.

> [8]Now come, write it on a tablet they can keep,
>   inscribe it on a scroll;
> That in time to come it may be
>   an eternal witness.
> [9]For this is a rebellious people,
>   deceitful children,

Children who refuse
    to listen to the instruction of the LORD;
[10]Who say to the seers, "Do not see";
    to the prophets, "Do not prophesy truth for
            us;
    speak smooth things to us, see visions that
            deceive!
[11]Turn aside from the way! Get
        out of the path!
    Let us hear no more
    of the Holy One of Israel!"

Isaiah had tirelessly urged his people to believe that the Lord was in charge of things. The preserved record (30:8) would reveal that disaster came because of the lack of acceptance and the foolishness involved in purely human pragmatic international politics.

The failure to accept the Lord's policy is reflected in the people's rejection of their prophets ("seers" is a synonym for prophets, those who see as God sees). In this rejection the people behave like children who will not heed the *torah*/instruction of their loving Lord who is the source of all wisdom (for similar rejection of instruction see Isa 1:10; 2:3; 5:24; 8:16). The refusal to listen to the Lord's *torah*/instruction is nothing less than rebellion. The forthcoming disaster stems from the people's imprudent and foolish policy. For them, the voice of the Holy One of Israel has been stilled.

¹²Therefore, thus says the Holy One of Israel:
   Because you reject this word,
And put your trust in oppression and deceit,
   and depend on them,
¹³This iniquity of yours shall be
   like a descending rift
Bulging out in a high wall
   whose crash comes suddenly, in an instant,
¹⁴Crashing like a potter's jar
   smashed beyond rescue,
And among its fragments cannot be found
   a sherd to scoop fire from the hearth
   or dip water from the cistern.

In addition to rejecting God's message through the prophet's words, the people have resorted to putting their trust in oppression and deceit. By such false trust Judah has committed itself not to the Lord's policy but to a policy entrenched in oppression and deceit. For Isaiah, these two policies are diametrically opposed. Only trust in the Lord, not purely pragmatic plans and programs, will result in stabilizing the imminent Assyrian threat.

The judgment comes in verses 13-14 where Isaiah resorts to graphic imagery. He paints a lurid picture of defeat and devastation in two graphic images: (1) the collapsing wall and (2) the broken pot.

When have you experienced the collapse of some false sense of security? Where did you turn for help?

Although the wall seems to be impregnable, it will come crashing down—like the successful siege of a city. Although one might hope that some shards of the pot could be salvaged, the pot is utterly and definitively beyond repair.

Here one does well to recall the metaphor of the Lord as potter and Judah as clay (see Isa 29:16). In its lack of trust Judah has unfortunately forgotten that the Lord as potter retains full freedom over the future of the clay. This seemingly ruthless destruction of the pot serves

as an example of that freedom. And to think that this calamity stems from Judah's refusal to trust the Lord and his policy!

[15]For thus said the Lord GOD,
   the Holy One of Israel:
By waiting and by calm you shall be saved,
   in quiet and in trust shall be your strength.
   But this you did not will.
[16]"No," you said,
   "Upon horses we will flee."
   Very well, you shall flee!
"Upon swift steeds we will ride."
   Very well, swift shall be your pursuers!
[17]A thousand shall tremble at the threat of one—
   if five threaten, you shall flee.
You will then be left like a flagstaff on a mountaintop,
   like a flag on a hill.

Here begins a new section of this unit that fleshes out the meaning of genuine *trust*. The opening verse spells out the nature of salvation and strength. Only by total reliance on the Lord, not on numbers and weapons, can Israel defeat its enemies. Judah's rush to purely military and political resources contradicts the "waiting" and "calm" of holy war strategy. Isaiah further develops these notions by speaking of "quiet" and "trust" as the formula for strength. All four terms in verse 15 bespeak utter reliance upon and total commitment to the Lord. Lacking these qualities and trusting in horses/steeds can only result in military disaster: "like a flagstaff on a mountaintop, / like a flag on a hill."

In Isaiah's view only trust triumphs over politics. One cannot help but be reminded of 1 John 5:4: "And the victory that conquers the world is our faith" (see also Isa 7:9).

> [18]Truly, the LORD is waiting to be gracious to you,
>   truly, he shall rise to show you mercy;
> For the LORD is a God of justice:
>   happy are all who wait for him!

This verse introduces the announcement of salvation. In other words the harsh treatment in the previous section is not the Lord's final word. The key word in this passage is "wait." However, the prophet uses the term in two senses. First, the Lord is waiting to do good to his people. He develops this divine intention by employing Israel's old covenant vocabulary, namely, "be gracious" and "show mercy" (see Exod 34:6). Isaiah strengthens God's proposal of renewal by adding "a God of justice." Hence the Lord will initiate

Isaiah's words call Judah to a level of trust that may seem foolish, naive, or impractical. When have you been encouraged to defy what seems logical and trust instead that God will show you a better way?

a strategy whereby Judah can free itself from exploitation and enjoy a full life as members of God's family. This God is a God of renewal! Second, the people must wait for him. God has his own timetable for reversing Israel's fate. Hence "wait" belongs to the nature of trust (see Isa 8:17).

[19]Yes, people of Zion, dwelling in Jerusalem,
   you shall no longer weep;
He will be most gracious to you when you cry out;
   as soon as he hears he will answer you.
[20]The Lord will give you bread in adversity
   and water in affliction.
No longer will your Teacher hide himself,
   but with your own eyes you shall see your Teacher,
[21]And your ears shall hear a word behind you:
   "This is the way; walk in it,"
   when you would turn to the right or the left.
[22]You shall defile your silver-plated idols
   and your gold-covered images;
You shall throw them away like filthy rags,
   you shall say, "Get out!"

> Psalm 27:14 indicates that waiting for the Lord requires courage. What does your experience teach you about this needed courage?

Many authors contend that verses 19-26 are not the work of Isaiah of Jerusalem but of a later hand who seeks to provide a message of hope in a completely different scenario. However, as the passage now stands in the book of Isaiah, it reveals the results of renewed trust and reengaged attentiveness to the Lord's plan.

The passage begins with an echo of what God's people do best in time of peril, namely, cry out to their Lord. As Exodus 2:23-25 shows, the machinery of renewal begins with a cry for help that stirs the Lord to action. This cry captures both their need and their trust. The divine response takes the form of *torah*/instruction. However, the Teacher does not indulge in academic learning as if in a school setting. Rather, this Teacher strikes a blow against his people's former resistance to reform and renewal. Such a program entails an outreach that means "bread in adversity / and water in affliction." Unlike the people who formerly had ears to hear but did not hear and eyes to see but did not see (Isa 6:9-10), this renewed community will now see their Teacher and hear his word. As a result, they will walk in the way of genuine change of heart by dismantling their false idols and scuttling their images.

> 23He will give rain for the seed
>   you sow in the ground,
> And the bread that the soil produces
>   will be rich and abundant.
> On that day your cattle will graze
>   in broad meadows;
> 24The oxen and the donkeys that till the ground
>   will eat silage tossed to them
>   with shovel and pitchfork.
> 25Upon every high mountain and lofty hill
>   there will be streams of running water.
> On the day of the great slaughter,
>   when the towers fall,

^{26}The light of the moon will be like the light of
   the sun,
   and the light of the sun will be seven times
      greater,
   like the light of seven days,
On the day the Lord binds up the wounds of his
   people
   and heals the bruises left by his blows.

The passage concludes with a new rehabilitated
creation reflecting divine grace and mercy. Here
fertility reigns supreme. The seed sown in the
ground will germinate owing to the abundant
rain and eventually provide rich and more than
sufficient bread. In addition,
animal husbandry will prosper.
The phrase "Upon every high
mountain and lofty hill" recalls
the pagan religions that the
prophets condemned (see Jer
2:20; 3:6; 17:2). But now the
people's change of heart results
in overflowing fertility ("streams
of running water"). However,
this new creation does not stop
there. The sun and the moon will
collaborate in a fashion that ban-
ishes all darkness and eliminates any and all
threats to life. The passage concludes with a
touching image of the Divine Healer. This God
who earlier punished his people by a series of
devastating blows now binds up their wounds
and heals their bruises.

Isaiah is, first and foremost, the indefatigable preacher of the word. Having assumed both the criticizing and energizing modes of the prophetic calling, he ceaselessly labors to announce God's ongoing presence in their midst. He is not a political scientist, although he correctly calculates the strength of the Assyrian forces and the weakness of Judah's military. He constantly urges the adoption of a pro-Lord plan, not the acceptance of an anti-Assyria strategy. His God is always "the Holy One of Israel" who anticipates the impact of such holiness on the people of Judah.

One can perhaps sum up Isaiah's prophetic stance as an all-encompassing trust in this "Holy One." For Isaiah, this is never a retreat to never-never land where only God assumes all responsibility. Instead, trust is a faith-driven expectation of divine involvement that, in turn, demands a response from Judah. Such trust does not disguise the formidable obstacles and dangers threatening the people. On the contrary, such trust opens up a vision of a God who has a plan that challenges purely pragmatic political posturing. It is a plan that demands waiting, rest, and quiet.

Such an approach does not eliminate the din of Assyria's military prowess. Rather, it throws into high relief an involved and caring God.

Sometimes it seems that God is slow to act or even deaf to people's needs. How can waiting, rest, and quiet become important spiritual tools?

Praying the Word / Sacred Reading

Use the following petitions for your prayer or as a springboard to add scenarios where you feel called to a greater trust in God. Where might you need the courage to more deliberately allow God to take charge?

When I am fearful and anxious	God, grant me stillness.
When I am tired of waiting	God, grant me endurance.
When I am rebellious	God, grant me humility.
Tempted to go my own way	I turn to God who directs my path.
Tempted to trust in civil power alone	I choose to find peace in God's plan.
Tempted to seek quick solutions	I choose to wait upon the Lord.
Tempted to anxiously plot and plan	I claim the time to rest in God.

Prepare my heart, O Lord, to face the dangers of our world with the kind of courage and trust that Isaiah speaks of to your people. Give me a community of believers who cling to your goodness, your truth, and your desires above all other things. Give me a trusting heart.

Living the Word

Isaiah the prophet urged God's people to rely more completely on the promises of God even in situations that seemed dangerous to their nation. Waiting, not passively but actively, is part of the lesson on trust. Is there a situation in your parish or local community where you might lend a hand while waiting for God's plan to be fully revealed? Perhaps your involvement in an area agency on poverty or literacy is a way that God will act on others' behalf.

God's Unfathomable Achievement in Christ

Invite God to assist you in your prayer and study. Then read the following passage from Paul's letter to the Romans.

Romans 8:31-39

³¹What then shall we say to this? If God is for us, who can be against us? ³²He who did not spare his own Son but handed him over for us all, how will he not also give us everything else along with him? ³³Who will bring a charge against God's chosen ones? It is God who acquits us. ³⁴Who will condemn? It is Christ [Jesus] who died, rather, was raised, who also is at the right hand of God, who indeed intercedes for us. ³⁵What will separate us from the love of Christ? Will anguish, or distress, or persecution, or famine, or nakedness, or peril, or the sword? ³⁶As it is written:

"For your sake we are being slain all the day;
we are looked upon as sheep to be slaughtered."

³⁷No, in all these things we conquer overwhelmingly through him who loved us. ³⁸For I am convinced that neither death, nor life, nor angels, nor principalities, nor present things, nor future things, nor powers, ³⁹nor height, nor depth, nor any other creature will be able to separate us from the love of God in Christ Jesus our Lord.

After a few moments of quietly pondering the selection from Romans 8:31-39, consider the background information offered below in "Setting the Scene."

Setting the Scene

Paul's letter to the Romans stands as the masterpiece of all his extant correspondence. While it is evidently a composition of massive substance, it captures to a great extent the core of his missionary message. Probably writing from Corinth around the year AD 58 and planning his final journey to Jerusalem, he expresses his intention of going to Rome and from there to new missionary territory in Spain. In this letter he intends to offer the Roman Christian community his understanding of the Gospel and its consequences. By so doing, he seeks to avoid any false and hostile views of himself and his message that may be current in Rome.

The passage considered below forms the conclusion of the second part of the letter, that is, chapters 5 through 8. The beginning (5:1-11) and the end (8:31-39) share similarity in content, notably, the role of hope (and hence trust) that rests upon the love of God. Paul insists that hope does not disappoint because of the love of God poured into the hearts of Christians through the Spirit (5:5). In 8:37 Paul insists that believers will overcome any and all obstacles "through him who loved us." Though the word "trust" does not appear in the conclusion of this central section, the entire passage exudes and is totally permeated with the reality of trust because of Christ's achievement.

What words or ideas do you associate with trust?

The structure of the passage is rather straight-forward. It consists of a series of rhetorical questions to which no answer is explicitly provided. However, the final statement declares that the answer to all these questions must be "nobody." Paul places the first question and its implied response in verses 31-32. The second question about bringing charges against God's elect comes in verse 33. The third question about possible condemnation surfaces in verse 34. The fourth and final question about possible separation from Christ's love emerges in verses 35-37. The concluding explanation that serves as a summary appears in verses 38-39. Because of God's love manifested in the death of his Son, there is more than ample room for trust. Divine love and human trust are irretrievably interlocked.

The entire passage will be considered a few verses at a time. Use the occasional questions for group discussion or for your own personal reflection.

Understanding the Scene Itself

³¹**What then shall we say to this? If God is for us, who can be against us? ³²He who did not spare his own Son but handed him over for us all, how will he not also give us everything else along with him?**

The opening phrase introduces an objection that one must quickly reject. In light of Paul's previous argument that, for example, Christ is the firstborn among many brothers/sisters and thus believers constitute his extended family, nobody can possibly oppose them. "God is for us" sums up the message of God's saving justice in the Gospel. "For us," in particular, calls to mind Jesus' saving death (5:6-8) that, as Paul insists, is the ultimate expression of divine love. No power on earth, therefore, can stand in the way.

In verse 32 Paul strengthens his argument by recalling Abraham's intention to sacrifice his son Isaac. "Did not spare his own Son" clearly alludes to Genesis 22:16: "because you acted as you did *in not withholding from me your son, your only one,* I will bless you. . . ." Unlike Abraham, however, God actually "handed him over for us all" and thereby provided incontestable proof that "God is for us." Paul must conclude (in question form) that, since God

has provided this very ultimate expression of love, he will do everything else along with him. The sacrificial gift of the Son in love assures everything else. Here Paul has clearly established the basis for trust.

[33] Who will bring a charge against God's chosen ones? It is God who acquits us. [34] Who will condemn? It is Christ [Jesus] who died, rather, was raised, who also is at the right hand of God, who indeed intercedes for us. [35] What will separate us from the love of Christ? Will anguish, or distress, or persecution, or famine, or nakedness, or peril, or the sword? [36] As it is written:

"For your sake we are being slain all the day; we are looked upon as sheep to be slaughtered."

[37] No, in all these things we conquer overwhelmingly through him who loved us.

At the beginning of both verses 33 and 34 Paul brings up two questions that deal respectively with bringing a charge and condemning. Paul argues that God acquits his chosen ones and, with regard to condemning, that Christ's death and resurrection now place him in a position to intercede for us rather than condemn. The entire argument here recalls Isaiah 50:7-9 (the third so-called Suffering Servant song). In that passage the contending parties litigate in God's presence while God performs the function of a judge who proclaims the Servant innocent. Paul sounds a note of victory by announcing immediately after Christ's death the triumph of the resurrection. The phrase "was raised" reveals that the Father is the agent of Christ's victory over death.

At the start of verse 35 Paul poses the question about possible separation from the love of Christ. For Paul, nobody can bring about such a separation (in 5:5 the Spirit has already poured God's love into the hearts of believers).

For the sake of argument, however, Paul lists seven possible agents of separation from anguish to the sword. In so doing, Paul continues the scene of the trial with these agents as accusers of God's chosen ones. Paul realizes that all these life-threatening perils impact believers in the present age. To this end he recalls the experience of Israel by citing Psalm 44:23. Like Israel in this moving lament, believers can appear to be sheep to be slaughtered. However, Paul counters the force of such tribulations by insisting that Christians super-defeat ("conquer overwhelmingly") such death-dealing agents through the unfathomable love of Christ.

It is a further instance of Paul's teaching that God's power is revealed in human frailty (see 2 Cor 12:8-10).

> Read Romans 8:35. What hardships would you include in a list of items that seem to pull you away from Christ?

> In what situations around the world are people in most need of hearing this powerful message of God's triumphant love?

38For I am convinced that neither death, nor life, nor angels, nor principalities, nor present things, nor future things, nor powers, 39nor height, nor depth, nor any other creature will be able to separate us from the love of God in Christ Jesus our Lord.

To proclaim his utmost confidence ("I am convinced"), Paul proceeds to enumerate all those occult, mysterious powers that the ancients generally considered hostile to humans. Here astrology plays a considerable role, not only among Romans and Greeks but also among Jews, such as the Essenes of the Dead Sea Scroll community. After the physical realities of death and life, Paul mentions angels, principalities, and powers, that is, those spiritual forces believed to preside over the material world but now conquered by Christ. Present and future things may be related to astrology—hence Christians have no need to rely on the "expertise" of astrologers. Height and depth embrace the worlds ruled by the spirits of these regions. Paul concludes that neither these forces nor any other creature can separate believers from the love that God has manifested in handing over his Son for them.

Paul clearly ends this central section of his letter with a note of celebration (see Rom 11:33-36). For Paul God did not say it with flowers but said it with his Son. In handing over his Son to death and then by raising him from the dead, the Father has not only demonstrated his power but also manifested his love. It is such love that provides the insuperable basis for believers' trust. Trust, therefore, for Paul, can never be a cerebral, artificial construct. Rather, trust is the capacity to overcome any and all obstacles because divine love has become tangible in the death and resurrection of Jesus.

If in Psalm 121 the vision of Jerusalem's walls and ultimately of the temple itself encourages profound trust, for Paul it must be the cross outside the city walls that symbolizes to the *n*th degree the Christian's ability to trust.

In Galatians 2:20 Paul offers his manifesto of trust: "the Son of God . . . has loved me and given himself up for me." The death of Jesus reveals the depth of divine love.

> *Trust is the capacity to overcome any and all obstacles because divine love has become tangible in the death and resurrection of Jesus.*

The believer can draw up his or her own list of all those hostile powers that plague human existence today, from the threat of nuclear warfare to the rapidly growing menace of Alzheimer's disease. In the face of such formidable foes the believer can and indeed must adopt the trusting stance of the apostle: "No, in all these things we conquer overwhelmingly through him who loved us."

In what tangible ways have you experienced God's love in the midst of hardship? Have you grown more trusting of God as a result?

Praying the Word / Sacred Reading

I say "Thank you, Father," for sending your son
　　as a pledge of your unconquerable love for us.
As my gratitude increases,
　　may I learn to continually trust in your goodness and mercy.
Open my eyes to see the signs of your protection
　　and allow me to grow in courage as I face the realities of a world
　　so often torn apart by hatred and mistrust.

Allow me to experience the power of your love
   so that I know in the deepest part of my spirit
     that with you I am able
  to conquer overwhelmingly all those barriers
    to your love.

Living the Word

The word "faith" comes from the Latin "fides," which also means "trust." The verb form is "fidere," which means "to trust." To have faith or be a faithful disciple means not only that we understand the content of our belief but that we are called to trust in God. When we put our faith into action we are exhibiting our trust in the God who made us, cares for us, directs us, and shapes us continually. The next time you recite the creed or make some other statement of faith, substitute "I trust" in place of "I believe" and see what difference it makes in your perspective, how it widens your understanding of faith.